LET'S GET TURTLES

BY MILLICENT E. SELSAM

DRAWINGS BY ARNOLD LOBEL

A Science I Can Read Book

HARPER & ROW, PUBLISHERS
NEW YORK, EVANSTON, AND LONDON

For

BILLY SCHILIT

and

GERALD FRIED,

the real Billy and Jerry

"A turtle is not a pet," said Jerry.

"Yes, it is," said Billy.

"No, it is not," said Jerry.

"I want a pet that wags its tail

when I get home."

"My mother won't let me

have a dog," Billy said.

"So what?" said Jerry.

"I think my mother will."

"Look, Jerry," asked Billy,

"are we friends?"

"Yes," said Jerry.

"Well," said Billy.

"Let's get the same pets.

Let's get turtles."

"Why turtles?" asked Jerry.

"Well, they don't bark," said Billy.

"No," said Jerry.

"But they don't wag their tails either."

Billy thought. Then he said,

"Turtles don't take up much room.

And they do not cost

as much as a dog."

"No," said Jerry.

"But fish do not take up much room.

And they do not cost much either."

"But I already had a goldfish,"
said Billy.
"Let's go to the pet store
to look at the turtles."
"Oh, all right," said Jerry.

Billy and Jerry went to the pet store.

They found the turtles.

Little green turtles were slipping

on and off a big rock in the tank.

"What kind of turtles are these?"

asked Billy.

"Red-ears," said the pet-store man.

"See the red mark

on each side of the head?"

"How much are they?" asked Jerry.

"Fifty cents each,"

said the pet-store man.

Billy said, "We will be back.

Save a few turtles for us."

Billy and Jerry walked home.

"Where will we keep the turtles?"
asked Jerry.

"I can use my old fish tank,"
said Billy.

"I will have to buy something,"
said Jerry.

The next day Billy and Jerry
went back to the pet store.

Billy bought two turtles.

Jerry bought two turtles
and a turtle bowl.

They went to Billy's house.

Billy got out the fish tank.

He put one inch of water in it.

He put a big rock in the center.

"What is the rock for?"

asked his mother.

"So the turtles can dry off, I guess,"

said Billy.

"Why do you have water in the tank

in the first place?" asked his mother.

"I don't know," said Billy.

"But they have water in the tank

at the pet store."

Jerry put water and a rock

in his turtle bowl.

"Now what do we do?" asked Billy.

"We should have asked

the pet-store man."

"Well," said Jerry, "let's go back."

Billy and Jerry went back

to the pet store.

"How do we take care

of the turtles?" Billy asked.

"I don't know much about turtles,"

said the pet-store man.

"But here is a book about them."

"How much?" asked Billy.

"Thirty-five cents,"

said the pet-store man.

"I'll take one," said Billy.

"And I have turtle food,"

said the pet-store man.

"How much?" asked Billy.

"Twenty-five cents."

"I'll take a box," said Billy.

"Me too," said Jerry.

"Wait a few days before you feed them,"

said the pet-store man.

"Let them get used to the new tank.

And change the water every few days."

Billy and Jerry went to Billy's house.

"Give me the book," said Jerry.

"Read about food," said Billy.

"All right," said Jerry. "Here it is."

WHAT TURTLES EAT

Some turtles eat small animals.

Some turtles eat animals and plants.

Some turtles eat only plants.

"What about red-ears?" asked Billy.

Jerry looked in the book.

"Red-ears, red-ears . . . here it is."

Red-eared turtles must eat under the water.

"That is why they need

water in the tank," said Billy.

Jerry read on.

Red-eared turtles eat worms, meat,

shrimp, fish, fruits, and vegetables.

"What about the turtle food

in the box?" asked Billy.

"Nothing here about that," said Jerry.

"Well, they call it turtle food.

So turtles must eat it," said Billy.

"We can try it," said Jerry.

When Billy's father came home,

Billy showed him the turtles.

"Well," said his father, "turtles!

I used to have turtles

when I was a boy."

"Do you know how

to take care of them?" asked Billy.

"I know a few things," said his father.

"Most of these pet turtles

come from warm places in the south.

The water in the tank should be warm.

The turtle's blood gets as warm

or as cold as the water it lives in."

18

"When I go into the water,

does my blood get as cold

as the water?" asked Billy.

"Try it," said his father.

"Try it when you take your bath."

"I'll take a bath now," said Billy.

His father came with two thermometers.

He put the longer thermometer

in the water.

"How cold is it?" he asked Billy.

"Cold!" said Billy.

"Look at the red line

near the numbers," said his father.

"I think it says 80," said Billy.

"Right," said his father.

"The water is 80 degrees.

Now put this thermometer

in your mouth."

"That's the one Mother uses

to see if I have a fever," said Billy.

He put the thermometer in his mouth.

"Keep quiet for a few minutes,"

said his father.

After three minutes Billy's father

read the thermometer.

"It says 98.6," he said.

"That's normal," said Billy.

"Yes," said his father.

"That's the temperature you have unless you are sick."

"And the water is only 80," said Billy.

"So I am warmer than the water."

Later, Billy and his father went to the tank.

Billy put the long thermometer into the water.

He looked at the red line.

"70," he said.

"Now can I take

the turtles' temperatures?"

"We don't have the right kind

of thermometer," said his father.

"Take my word for it,

the turtles are about 70 degrees too.

The water for these turtles should be

between 75 and 85 during the day

and not below 65 at night."

"How do I keep it that way?"

asked Billy.

"I forgot how we did that,"

said his father.

In the morning Billy went to the tank.

Billy looked at the thermometer.

"65!" he said.

"My turtles must be 65 too."

After lunch Billy looked at

the thermometer again. "70," he said.

"That is not warm enough."

Billy went to see Jerry.

He took the thermometer with him.

"How are your turtles?" asked Billy.

"Look fine," said Jerry.

Jerry's turtle bowl

was on the windowsill.

The sun was shining.

"Do you know how warm

your turtles are?" asked Billy.

"No. Do you?" asked Jerry.

Billy took the thermometer

from his pocket.

He put it in the water.

"90!" he said.

"Your turtles are almost

as warm as you are."

"How warm am I?" asked Jerry.

"You are always 98.6

unless you are sick.

"But a turtle's temperature," said Billy,

"is the same as the water's temperature.

"Do you know how cold

my turtles were this morning? 65!"

"How do you know?" asked Jerry.

"The water was 65," said Billy.

"And my father says a turtle's

temperature is the same as the water."

"Why didn't you take

the turtles' temperatures?" asked Jerry.

"I wish I could have," said Billy.

"But we did not have
the right thermometer."
"Why do you want to know how warm
the turtles are anyway?" asked Jerry.
"My father says these turtles
come from warm places.
They must be kept warm," said Billy.
"My turtles are warm," said Jerry.
"They are 90 now."

"That is too warm," said Billy.

"The sun is making the water too hot.

But see what happens tonight."

"All right," said Jerry.

"Leave your thermometer here."

The next morning Jerry looked

at the thermometer.

"55!" he cried.

He called Billy on the telephone.

"My turtles are too cold now," he said.

"Take the bowl off the windowsill,"

said Billy.

"The water gets too hot there

during the day.

And it gets too cold at night."

"All right, I'll move them,"

said Jerry.

"But are your turtles

the right temperature?"

31

"No," said Billy.

"The water goes down to 65 at night.

That is all right.

But it only goes to 70 during the day.

And that is too cold.

The water should be

between 75 and 85 then."

"How do you know

what the water should be?"

asked Jerry.

"My father told me," said Billy.

"But he can't remember

how to keep it that way."

"Let's go to the pet store

and see how they do it," said Jerry.

Billy and Jerry met at the pet store.

There was a thermometer

in the turtle tank.

It said 85.

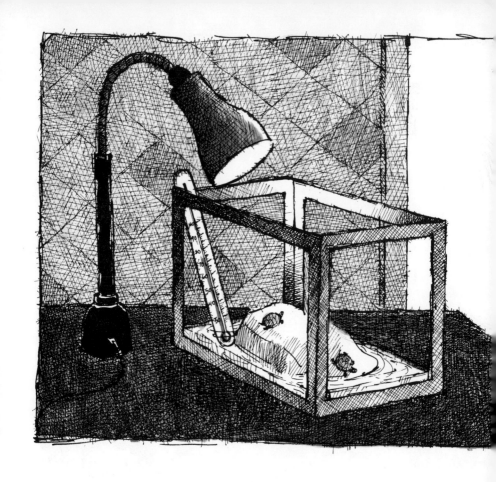

"That light in the tank must be keeping the water warm," said Jerry.

"We could put a light over our turtles."

"I'll try it," said Billy.

"Me too," said Jerry.

That afternoon Billy put a lamp

over his tank.

He put the thermometer into the water.

Later he looked at it.

"75. It works!" he said.

He called Jerry on the telephone.

"Did yours work?" he asked.

"I think so," said Jerry.

"The water feels warm.

But bring your thermometer."

Billy took his thermometer

to Jerry's house.

He put it in the turtle bowl.

"80! These lamps work fine," he said.

"At night we'll turn them off.

But if it gets very cold in the house,

we can leave the lights on all night."

"Good idea!" said Jerry.

The next day Jerry called Billy.

He said,

"Now our turtles are warm enough.

But isn't it time we fed them?"

"Yes," said Billy.

"I'm going to try turtle food,"

said Jerry.

"I'm going to try fish," said Billy.

Jerry took some turtle food

from the box.

He put it in the turtle bowl.

The turtles did not move.

Jerry picked up a turtle.

He put it near the food.

The turtle moved away.

He picked up the other turtle.

He put it near the food.

The turtle touched the food

with its mouth.

Then it moved away.

"Now what?" thought Jerry.

"I can't stay here all day.

How will I know if the turtles eat?

I know. I will count the pieces."

There were six pieces.

Jerry went away.

He came back an hour later.

There were still six pieces.

The next day there were still six pieces.

The turtles were not eating.

Jerry went to Billy's house.

"Did your turtles

eat the fish?" he asked.

"Yes," said Billy.

"Watch me and I'll show you how."

He went to the kitchen and got a roll.

He put the roll

at the edge of the table.

"Now I'm a turtle," he said.

"I come along under the water.

I grab the roll with my mouth.

Now I push with one hand.

Now I push with the other hand.

Now I have a piece of roll in my mouth.

I swallow it.

Then I grab the roll

in my mouth again.

And I push with one hand."

"Stop!" cried Jerry.

"That's enough. But listen.

My turtles did not eat anything."

"Then try fish," said Billy.

Jerry got some fish from the fish store.

He cut it up into little pieces.

He put some in the turtle bowl.

One turtle came along.

It touched the fish with its mouth.

Then it moved away.

The other turtle came along.

It touched the fish with its mouth.

Then it moved away.

"Now what will I do?"

Jerry asked his mother.

"These turtles will not even eat fish!"

"Well, take out the fish anyway,"

said his mother.

"It will make the water smell

if it stays there too long.

That is one thing I know."

The next day Jerry tried ground meat.

The turtles did not eat it.

Then he tried a piece of banana.

The turtles did not eat it.

Each time he took out the uneaten food.

He wanted to keep the turtle bowl clean.

But his turtles were not eating.

Jerry went to see Billy.

"What shall I do, Billy?" he asked.

"My turtles will not eat anything!"

"Let's call the zoo," said Billy.

"They have lots of turtles there.

They will know what to do."

Billy asked his mother to call the zoo.

"Please let me talk," said Jerry.

"All right," said Billy's mother.

She called the zoo.

"May I please speak to someone
who knows about turtles?" she said.

Then she gave the phone to Jerry.

"Hello," he said.

"Can you tell me why
my turtles will not eat?"

He listened.

When Jerry hung up, Billy asked,

"What did they say?"

"The man said to try some live worms,"
said Jerry.

"He said I can get them
at the pet store."

"Go right home," said Billy.

"I will be there in a minute."

In a few minutes

Jerry's doorbell rang.

It was Billy.

"Here is a present," he said.

He took the lid off a paper cup.

Inside there were little red worms.

"Try some," said Billy.

Jerry put a few worms in the bowl.

Jerry and Billy sat quietly.

One turtle was moving.

Its long neck stuck out of its shell.

It stopped.

Then its mouth opened

and, snap, one worm was gone.

The turtle moved along.

Snap! Another worm was gone.

Billy and Jerry looked at each other.

"It's working! It's working!"

cried Jerry.

"My troubles are over."

For a week Jerry gave worms

to his turtles.

They ate every one.

Then he started to give them

other things to eat.

52

He gave them fish. They ate it.

He gave them meat. They ate it.

"My turtles are eating everything!"

he said to his mother.

"You ought to call the man at the zoo
and thank him," she said.

"Call him for me, please," said Jerry.

His mother called the zoo.

She asked for the keeper of the turtles.

"Hello," said Jerry. "This is Jerry.
Remember?

I called you about my turtles?

You told me to give them worms.

Well, it worked.

Now my turtles are eating everything."

He turned to his mother.

"The man at the zoo says to come
and see their turtles."

"We will go on Sunday,"

said his mother.

"Let's take Billy," said Jerry.

On Sunday, Billy and Jerry went
to the zoo.

They found the turtle house.

They asked to see the turtle keeper.

"Tell him it's Jerry," said Jerry.

A man came out.

"Which one is Jerry?" he asked.

"Here I am," said Jerry.

"And this is Billy.

He has turtles too."

"I am glad your turtles

are eating now,"

said the man.

"I want to ask you something,"

said Jerry.

"Why don't turtles eat

turtle food from the box?"

58

"Some do," said the turtle keeper.

"But the food in the box

is mostly dried flies.

Turtles need more food than that.

We give our baby turtles fish,

cut up into little pieces,

and ground meat.

That makes a good turtle dinner.

We feed it to them

three times a week."

"That is what I am going to do,"

said Billy.

"Me too," said Jerry.

"And by the way,"

said the turtle keeper,

"we add bone meal to the meat."

"What is that for?" asked Jerry.

"To help the shell grow," said the man.

"Where can we get it?" asked Jerry.

"At the five-and-ten," said the man.

"A little cod liver oil helps too.

Vitamins, you know."

Billy and Jerry looked at each other.

Then the turtle keeper said,

"Why don't you try something for me?

"Jerry, you give your turtles

the turtle dinner.

Add a pinch of bone meal to the meat.

Billy, you do the same.

But add a drop of cod liver oil

to the meat once a week."

Billy and Jerry were quiet.

Then Billy said,

"Is this an experiment?"

"Yes," said the turtle keeper.

"Let me know what happens, will you?"

A month later Jerry wrote a letter

to the turtle keeper.

It said:

Dear TurtleKeeper,
Billy and I are doing what you said. His turtles and mine still look about the same. We can't be sure though. We should have measured when we started our experiment. We measured them today. We will write again in a few weeks.
your friend,
Jerry